YOUR KNOWLEDGE HAS VALUE

Katrin Schmidt

'European Integration since 1945 has contributed to saving rather than undermining the European nation state' - A discussion

GRIN Verlag

Bibliografische Information der Deutschen Nationalbibliothek:

Die Deutsche Bibliothek verzeichnet diese Publikation in der Deutschen National-
bibliografie; detaillierte bibliografische Daten sind im Internet über http://dnb.d-
nb.de/ abrufbar.

Imprint:

Copyright © 2005 GRIN Verlag GmbH
Druck und Bindung: Books on Demand GmbH, Norderstedt Germany
ISBN: 978-3-640-11372-9

This book at GRIN:

http://www.grin.com/en/e-book/94221/european-integration-since-1945-has-contri-
buted-to-saving-rather-than

GRIN - Your knowledge has value

Der GRIN Verlag publiziert seit 1998 wissenschaftliche Arbeiten von Studenten, Hochschullehrern und anderen Akademikern als eBook und gedrucktes Buch. Die Verlagswebsite www.grin.com ist die ideale Plattform zur Veröffentlichung von Hausarbeiten, Abschlussarbeiten, wissenschaftlichen Aufsätzen, Dissertationen und Fachbüchern.

Visit us on the internet:

http://www.grin.com/

http://www.facebook.com/grincom

http://www.twitter.com/grin_com

European Integration since 1945 has contributed to saving rather than

undermining the European nation state. Discuss.

European integration has been undergoing a special development recently. 2005 has

been a decisive year for the future of the European Union and its member states. The

draft of the Constitutional Treaty due to be ratified by the European member states has

not been accepted by the Dutch and the French people. What impact do those decisions

have on the European nation state? Do they state that European integration has saved

the nation state implying that there will be no future federal European state? In what

way has European integration undermined the nation state since 1945?

The nation state can be defined as "a specific form of state, which exists to provide a

sovereign territory for a particular nation, and derives its legitimacy from that function.

In the ideal model of the nation-state, the population consists of the nation and *only* of

the nation: the state not only houses it, but protects it and its national identity" (website

1).

After World War II most European nation states were in a disastrous situation as far as

their national identity, the economic and political situation were concerned.

Economically the nation states suffered from the world's recession, inflation and

unemployment. The situation was so insecure that Rose (1996, p. 42) draws an analogy to Weimar Germany where the uncertain political circumstances (lack of belief in democracy) triggered World War II.

In 1945 the continent was split into two antagonist political, socio-economic and military blocks which led to the period of Cold War (1949-1981/91). The Western countries founded NATO (North Atlantic Treaty Organisation) in 1948 as an antagonist to the communist countries which aligned to the Warsaw Pact in 1955. At the same time an end of the European nation states' power over their colonies could be observed. Another trend was the beginning of a first European movement (see website 2). Priority after the Second World War was given to the "creation of a viable frame work for international trade and finance" (Gillingham 2003, p. 73). For the same reason the treaty of the ECSC (European Coal and Steel Community) was signed in 1951, to make sure that the European nation states profit as much as possible from coal and steel production which was one of the most important branches and put large parts of the unemployed post-war population back to work. Although the ECSC was founded for economic reasons it later became a basic element of the EEC (European Economic Community).

A bigger step towards European integration was the union of ECSC and EURATOM (European Atomic Energy Community) to the EEC by signing the Treaty of Rome in 1957. A new body of European constitutional law with the power to override national courts was created. Symbolically the signing nation states transferred part of their sovereignty to the EEC. Only a few years after World War II the opposing nation states became equal partners and founded their own economic community. That the community did not only focus on economic matters but dealt increasingly with political and other affairs were proven when media and literature got rid of the adjective "economic" during the 1970s and the EEC linguistically became the EC (European Community). The 1950s and 1960s turned out to be decades of economic growth all over Europe. Therefore it was easier for the nation states to think in terms of European Community and to push the integration process forward instead of concentrating on national matters only.

The Nation states regained their power during the following recession in the 1970s, which was triggered by the collapse of the Bretton Woods system. This period was also described as decade of Keynesian ascendancy (see Gillingham 2003, p. 81). The economist Keynes demanded a strong state. He advised governments to use its fiscal and monetary policy to help eliminate recessions and control economic booms. Concerned with the idea of a strong nation state the pace of European integration slowed down again.

Generally it can be said that in times of economic growth the integration process develops faster than in times of economic recessions. During recessions nation states become stronger since their citizens confront them directly by demanding a solution of the recession. European integration thus rather undermines the nation state but when it comes to situations in which a strong national focus is demanded nation states regain their power. It cannot be denied that those economic crises were even strengthened by the Europeanization (the assimilation into European culture, see website 5) and respectively the economic interdependence.

The first enlargement of the EC took place in 1973 when Denmark, the United Kingdom and Ireland joined the EC. This enlargement was not threatening, was no economic burden, because those countries were economically almost as strong as the former six. The following enlargements of Greece (1981), Portugal and Spain joining the EU in 1986 meant a greater responsibility for all member states which committed themselves to help each other economically.

The basis of the "rescue of the nation state" (Milward 1994, p. 44) was an economic one, which suggests that the Europeanization of its rescue had also to be economic. Milward states that the "interdependence of European states was, however, by no means purely economic (ibid.)". In his view Germany's political future was the "greatest problem within that interdependence" (ibid.). After the Second World War the independent development of West Germany was seen as a motor and model for Europe. The result was a "different Germany in Europe" (Gillingham 2003, p. 76). The new progress of European integration was not dominated by anyone but was rather an example of interdependence. The German unification in 1990 meant a threat to this stability. The GDR automatically became a member of the EC. Other nation states feared a dominant role of Germany, which was stressed by the historical experience of the Second World War. Conservative M.P. John Redwood expressed his own anxieties on the issue in an article taken from *The Times*: "I will never feel loyalty to a government in which Germany has the most powerful voice. Nor will I feel sufficiently European to accept the authority of a European flag and government over my loyalty to my country, the U.K."

The Maastricht Treaty came into effect in 1993. The EC was supplemented by the CFSP (Common Foreign and Security Policy) and the Justice and Home Affairs pillars. Besides, a common currency, the Euro, was created. This system of pillars is called intergovernmental in contrast to supranational. The nation states did not want to give away their main power to a supranational organisation but they realised the necessity of combining their powers in certain issues as security policy for instance. Although the ratification process took some time and was in some cases only carried by small majorities (e.g. referendum in France), the Maastricht Treaty was a big step in the direction of European integration. The opening of the Channel Tunnel in 1994 can be interpreted as a symbol for European integration for it links the nation states closer and faster to each other. Austria, Sweden and Finland joined the EU in 1995. Norway's population voted against becoming a member of the EU.

In 1997 the member states signed the Treaty of Amsterdam. The Amsterdam Treaty supplements and clarifies some areas of the Maastricht Treaty, e.g. national and European citizenship. The European citizenship is to complement and not replace the national citizenship (see website 4). Citizenship is not only a formal matter. Although there are a lot of additional rights given to European citizens, the identification only takes place if people travel through Europe or move into a different nation state to work and live there. The possibilities to do so were established by the treaties. Now it is time for the European citizens to experience being Europeans. As long as they mainly identify with their nation states Europe will only be a theoretical construction.

The ECB (European Central Bank) was established in 1998. It is situated in Frankfurt am Main in Germany. The establishment of the ECB lead to the redundancy of the nation states' national banks. The Euro was introduced as currency in 1999, three years later its notes and coins followed. Today the Euro has completely replaced most national currencies. But especially old people still identify with the former currencies and convert the Euro into their former currencies when shopping. But younger (and future generations) identify stronger with the Euro and enjoy the advantage of having only one European currency when travelling. Despite all fears of a weak stability the Euro is accepted and enjoys a stable reputation worldwide. Peter Evans' statement: "Economic globalization does restrict State power but transnational capital needs capable States as much (or more) than does domestically oriented business" (Vercauteren 2001, p. 13) can be applied to the EU saying that the success of the Euro is dependent on the success of European integration. If the European nation states trust in the new currency and show this trust to their economic partners, the Euro can resist monetary markets fluctuations. From the economic perspective nation states' economies are so interwoven within the EU that an autonomous existence of a nation states' economy is not imaginable anymore (see Vercauteren 2001, p.34).

Although there is one European currency, still twenty official languages (Spanish, Danish, German, Greek, English, French, Italian, Dutch, Portuguese, Finnish, Swedish, Czech, Estonian, Latvian, Lithuanian, Hungarian, Maltese, Polish, Slovak, Slovene, Irish will become the 21st official language in 2007, website 5) exist within the EU.

The Treaty of Nice was signed in 2001. Its aim was to amend the former treaties in order to further the European operational policy more. It dealt mainly with new quotes for majorities in the process of decision making. Lithuania, the Czech Republic, Cyprus, Estonia, Hungary, Latvia, Malta, Poland, Slovakia and Slovenia became members of the EU in 2004. Their membership started severe discussions about the common agricultural policy and similar issues. The EU is confronted with new challenges in decision making as well. For the European identity the enlargement is also challenging. There might occur identity problems as well because people from western European countries do not share the political past with eastern European countries. As the EU has immensely enlarged many nation states might focus more on their own issues again. A recent discussion about increasing the European budget has lead to recriminations. The impact of the latest enlargement on the European identity will be determined in future.

The challenge of globalisation has led to Europeanization. From the economic perspective the EU has become one of the most important agents. Politically the EU still consists of interdependent nation states rather than one union. In what way has European integration saved or undermined the nation state? Erikson and Fossum (2000, p. 3) describe the nation state as "Janus-faced" which faces its domestic arena as well as the EU and might be torn apart between them. Integration has definitely led to the partial giving up of national sovereignty of the European nation states. But sovereignty in the most important matters still lies with the nation states. Only in sectors where cooperation is absolutely necessary like security policy, nation states have transferred large parts of their power to the EU. Rose (1996, p. 264) claims that Europe is not a state because its nation states are still important. Europe lacks its own military force and the revenue-raising powers of a nation state, although there has been a decline of national defence in terms of national service and defence budgets in the last years. Another factor which is important for the establishment of a European identity is the fact that there is no single European capital. Whereas Germans clearly identify with Berlin, European citizens might be torn between Brussels, Strasbourg, Amsterdam, Kirchberg and Frankfurt where the European institutions are located and Rome, Nice, Maastricht and Amsterdam where most important European treaties were signed. The importance the Supreme Court might have for American media and citizens cannot be observed with European institutions. In relation to its responsibilities "the institutions of the EU are light weighted" (Rose 1996, 264) in terms of power, budget and staff. On the other hand the EU is more substantial than other international bodies, e.g. NATO. The Rome and Maastricht Treaties give power to act and bind member states to its decisions. But in case of inflation and deficit spending in Germany and France, the EU has deviated from its principles and has not fined the nation states. That the EU is more supranational than NATO can also be seen by its "multiplicity of policies" (Rose 1996, p. 264). As long as the European identity is still lacking a "democratic self-consciousness of its collective citizen body, emphasising of shared 'belief-systems', public awareness of integration processes, determination to direct democratic claims to the central institutions and a 'sense of community' to support concerted civic activities" (Vercauteren 2001), the process of European integration is still going on.

The conflicting theories of the European federalists and the Anti-Europeans will always exist. European integration will save the European nation state and improve the interdependent policy of the EU. In times of crises (e.g. massive unemployment) nation states will refresh their power because their citizens will rather lean to the national governments than to the European institutions.

A change of this balance between the supranational EU and the nation states might be activated when (and if) the Constitutional Treaty will be ratified by all European member states. So far European integration has not undermined the nation states.

Bibliography:

Books:

ERIKSEN, E.O. and FOSSUM, J.E., ed., 2000. *Democracy in the European Union. Integration trough Delibaration?* London: Routledge.

GILLINGHAM, J., 2003. *European integration, 1950-2003: superstate or new market economy?* Imprint. Cambridge: Cambridge University Press.

MILWARD, A. S., 1994. *The European Rescue of the Nation-State.* London: Routledge.

ROSE, R., 1996. *What is Europe?: a dynamic perspective.* Imprint. New York: HarperCollins College Publishers.

Newspapers and Journals:

REDWOOD, J., 1996. *Saving Europe from itself.* The Times, 29/3/1996, p.18

VERCAUTEREN, P., 2001. *European Integration and the Crisis of the State.* Queen's Papers on Europeanization, No. 7/2001

Internet resources:

website1: http://en.wikipedia.org/wiki/Nation-state (6/11/2005) website 2: http://www.bbc.co.uk/history/war/wwtwo/legacy_01.shtml (31/10/2005)

website 3: http://www.thefreedictionary.com/Europeanisation (9/11/2005)

website 4: http://europa.eu.int/scadplus/leg/en/lvb/a12000.htm (9/11/2005)

website 5: http://europa.eu.int/comm/education/policies/lang/languages/index_en.html (9/11/2005)

website 6: http://education.ntu.ac.uk/resources/ict_resources/EuroDim/Nationalism/ Union.html (31/10/2005)